A Poet's
Shabbat E

C000262986

Liturgy through the eyes of poets
edited by Rick Lupert

A Poet's Siddur

Shabbat Evening

Ain't Got No Press

Design and Layout ~ Rick Lupert

agnp@poetrysuperhighway.com

or

www.poetrysuperhighway.com/agnp

First Edition ~ First Printing ~ November, 2017

ISBN: 978-0-9820584-8-0 $18.00

CONTENTS

Adon Olam

Motzi

Introduction

I've become more and more enchanted with the left side of the page. Specifically I'm referring to the tradition of newer *siddurim* (prayerbooks) complementing the traditional prayers and liturgy, which, in these new volumes, appear on the right side of the page, with alternate texts on the left facing pages. These alternate texts, which you might find in the Reform movement's *Mishkan T'filah*, or the Conservative movement's *Siddur Sim Shalom*, provide a sometimes modern, and sometimes ancient interpretation, or re-interpretation of the traditional text on the right. The old becomes new, giving the new the chance to become holy.

I'm reminded of the *this isn't the right melody* controversy. (And I'm not a hundred percent sure *controversy* is the right word here.) Have you ever been at a synagogue for a prayer service and found a familiar melody to a prayer had changed? Sometimes new melodies can feel foreign or uncomfortable. (until you hear them four times which is the official exact number of times that converts a new melody into an old one. [don't believe everything you read]) But for the person who wrote or chose that melody, it was the *exact* right one. These new notes or musical modality allowed the composer to connect with the prayer in a way that was right for them. This has been going on forever. Many of the melodies considered "traditional" were written within the last hundred years or so...mere babies in the greater longevity of the texts they're accompanying.

Enter poets; rabbi poets, cantor poets, famous Canadian singer-songwriter poets, regular citizens of poetry, all trying to figure out what the details of this journey between birth and death mean... sending every image and experience through their own unique filter, until stanzas and line breaks come out the other side. *Jewish* stanzas and linebreaks.

In *A Poet's Sidder: Shabbat Evening* the included authors revere, reinterpret, and down-right struggle with our liturgy. All of this is as it should be. Our name is *Israel* after all. We are literally defined as strugglers. We're meant to wrestle with our tradition and not always win. You may be saying the Mi Chamocha one day and find you are actually feeling the mud on your feet as we walk across the open channel between walls of water. The very next day it might occur to you *walls of water? Are they kidding? They must have misunderstood a tsunami.*

Don't get me wrong; not every poem in this collection is a *struggler*. Some of them are loving rides along the intended *kavanah* of the original text. Some of them are deeply personal explorations of the themes and imagery of their companion prayers. The *strugglers* and the *celebrators* sit side by side on these pages like every family reunion – meant to be together even if sometimes they don't talk.

My hope is that these poems encourage an ongoing conversation between you and our liturgy. Whether you accent prayers in a Friday evening service with a piece from here, or you read it like any old-fashioned poetry anthology, this conversation is never meant to end. I mean, like, *never*. This is the conversation we inherited...and this is the conversation our children, if we're so lucky, will inherit.

So write on, and read on, and pray on. Every Jewish thought is a future *Mishnah*.

Rick Lupert
November 1, 2017
Van Nuys, California

"Prayer is translation. A man translates himself into a child asking for all there is in a language he has barely mastered."

Leonard Cohen

CANDLES

Erev Shabbat Far From Home

by Ellen Sander

Sunset at Shabbat in
South beaches
Mother's voice and
Candles at sunset on Friday.

Just for one moment
Think peace and it hovers
Like a gull in the air
Before it drops a bomb.

A Prayer (Not found in the Siddur)

by David Supper

I remember when, so many years ago,
Friday nights were special
just because my Mother lit the candles,
Waved her hands and mumbled
The prayer to welcome shabbas.

Those were the days when religion
Was no stranger to me,
And I could join with others of my faith
To spend a morning in the shul,
Though I never learnt to doven.

My post-Barmitzvah years
Were largely spent in teenage revolt
Against the dogma of the faith,
And the hours sitting in the synagogue
Bring memories I'd rather soon forget.

The blue stained copy of the siddur,
Eagerly passed from hand to hand,
Each supplicant licked a grimy finger
And scanned through pages at a pace,
Until he found the place and could begin.

I always kept my copy open
The page was always happenstance,
Unless a 'kindly' worshipper, by chance,
Should lean across and show me where we were,
Embarrassed I would flick my Tallit, and pretend to pray.

'Please God (do you exist?) forgive me these transgressions,
I do not understand why this is so important. Ormain.'

Blessing over the candles

by Janet Bowdan

Blessed are you, Bringer of light, who gave us sun and also
clouds to cover the sun and also evening for the light to slip
away (or *dive [said at the equator]*) gorgeously below the
horizon; who gave us occasion to bring this small flame into
our lives, a reminder of the day.

[Optional: Blessed are you, Protector of light, who keeps
the cats' interested noses far from the flame, and also
their paws, which otherwise might tip the candles into
the curtains. Blessed are you who keep upright the wobbly
candlesticks made by the eldest child in her *Gan* art class and
who defendest the paper placemat designed by the youngest
child to catch the wax drips.]

Candle Lighting <small>by I.B. Iskov</small>

I am self-taught in the art
of memorized magic
ancient incantations
ignite in a moment,
bloom at once.
Bright yellow flickering petals
spike halos,
run off into the air.

My grandmother would be proud
again and again,
lighting her candlesticks,
praying respectfully
with mellowed hands
weighted with worries
beneath salt water and scars.

My Hebrew is a pretense
I have created myself
wrapped in a Canadian shawl
on a dead end street,
moving lips in moral denial.

A thick fabric of warmth
shades precious
still.

Stretching the Light by Neal Whitman

Added
to
the bliss
of kindling
is its care-taking.
We can make the light last longer
if we learn how to trim its wick.
We, too, need pruning,
as we grow
to serve
our
Lord.

Illumine by Joanne Jagoda

Le Hadlik Ner
Like the myriads before me
as strong as lionesses
we have kept the fires of our faith burning
candles lit in hidden cellars
concealed in shtetels and ghettos
now standing at my kitchen counter
with familiar age-old motions
my hands draw the precious light to my face
the spirit of our foremothers
surrounds me
now my little ones
watch your grandmother
as I kindle the Sabbath candles
carry on this tradition
the spark of our identity
Oh G-d, renew us and fill us with the spirit of Shabbat
bless my household with sweetness and good health
bring us peace and contentment
Le Hadlik Ner

The Candle by Don Schaeffer

After all this,
it really is all about
breathing. Each inflation
is faith, awaiting
the materials of the planet.
Each exhale is a prayer.
I give you
what is in my body
knowing how the world
is large and generous.
We are made to pray.
We hang on the planet
like prayer machines,
in and out in prayer rotation.
We don't need to know and figure,
we don't need the words.

KABBALAT
SHABBAT

Dolphin Sabbath   by Florence Weinberger

Most times the dolphins show up, summoned,
the rabbi says, by our singing,
our hot skin, Sabbath candles lit and sunk snugly in the sand,
sweet wine to bless the week to come.
In kinship, they sing with us,

they who have taught surfers their leap up
and glide home. But what of days we worship
and find ourselves rebuffed, the water's surface dull as mud.
I want to believe a holy desire can draw the dolphins back
to show us their constancy,

their fearless dependency on the tides of plenty,
their dumb trust that they will always ride the crest of new birth.
Of course we were fish;
raising our heads, we sang to the heavens, sang
as we groped our way to shore on our small unbinding feet.

You'd Sing Too   by Leonard Cohen

You'd sing too
if you found yourself
in a place like this
You wouldn't worry about
whether you were as good
as Ray Charles or Edith Piaf
You'd sing
You'd sing
not for yourself
but to make a self
out of the old food
rotting in the astral bowel
and the loveless thud
of your own breathing
You'd become a singer
faster than it takes
to hate a rival's charm
and you'd sing, darling
you'd sing too

Chuppah by Adam D. Fisher

Fine-boned fingers and branches barely touch

as they   arch across

the road   toward one

another   forming a

chuppah   for the

       Shechinah and me.

Come, Greet the Bride by Harris Gardner

Places, lights, no cameras.
The music begins, no organ.
No orchestra. All voices soar
In perfect pitch. All rise and
Turn toward the door.

So eager are the guests
To greet the perpetual Bride.
Her beauty builds legends-
Graceful, spirited, bright,
A delight for the ages.

Candlelight flickers,
Drawn toward an unseen hand.
Oh, the anticipation !
A murmur ripples the congregation.

She's here, oh, she's here !
We bow and bid her welcome.
No need for the photographer.
We can picture her always.

This twenty-four hour ceremony
Lasts forever. The invites are open-
Ended. You are always on the list.
No one is perfect, except the Bride.

Lekah Dodi   by Alan Walowitz

I have welcomed my beloved
too many times to think of this as new.
Yet here I am again, at what ought to be beginning,
back turned to the week, face to the door,
hardly richer for the settlements I have made,
the sum of all mistakes that've come before,
bills paid and too many left with a sigh, unopened.
The phone's rung off the hook unanswered and insistent
though your voice that follows so often
reminds me that my presence is long overdue.
I have heard you promise, the wretched week will fade to the past
but not until I hear the footsteps in the distance
that rise like a gentle wave on the beach at dusk, will I believe.
Ah, the subtle music, the fragrance, then open your eyes--
a celebrant she comes and will I only have the will
to go and meet her, look beneath the veil
and ready myself to embrace the joy
that ought to be mine by birthright.

Pictures at an Exhibition: Shabbat

by Seree Cohen Zohar

I sing for you, I trawl the souq, I croon to you,
the week tingles of readying, my stocking up
for you — have I sinned lavishly? —

for I covet you, each crowded night since you left
a pool of expectation, each bluing daybreak
counting out the certainty of return,

wending your tapered way through clouds,
splendor the robe you wear, weaved of eve's
sidling, unwound from spools of carmine

and plum; I am the laden table set for you,
the candles lighted for you, loved one; six days
it's taken you until, thrilled by your whisper

at the doorway, I say, "At last, beloved; come
inside; did my flickering illumine your way?
At last here we are, alone, again; my man has gone

to pray; but you have come to sit beside me,
encape my shoulders as you always do,
and milky your touch brushing my waist

where my fresh-washed hair honeys down my back for you."

Welcoming the Sabbath Bride

by Joanne Jagoda

Lecho Dodi Likrat Kaloh
the golden sun fades
we shut off I-phones, dim computer screens
stillness descends with stuttering reticence
eagerly waiting for you, Sabbath bride
to cross our threshold
anticipating your grand entrance
growing impatient like petulant children
yearning for the sweet light you bring
Sabbath bride, exquisite one
heal the fissures of our broken week-day hearts
strained by the realities of this crazy world
slow the hectic pace of our lives
even for these few hours
as we revel in your gifts
elevate our ordinary souls
help us ascend your ladder to the sublime
fill us with the shining spirit of the Divine
infuse us with the delight of the Sabbath
which has forever sustained our people
like the most precious manna
let us taste a morsel of the world to come
Sabbath bride, we welcome you
with wide-open arms
Lecho Dodi Likrat Kaloh

Welcome Shalom Aleikhem #1

by Rabbi James Stone Goodman

The operative word
The *le* of direction
Boachem le-shalom
Come to peace
Toward peace might be better
Not in peace that would be *b'shalom* --

We have learned to read
From the most clever readers and we notice right away
The lowly preposition
Only there are no lowly parts of speech for us
For we have learned to read from masters of words,

And we trip right away over l'shalom toward peace
So with *barkhuni le-shalom*
Bless us toward peace
It's like a dream it's like a vision it's like a blessing
And when you leave
Tzeit-khem le-shalom
Leave toward peace;

Always toward because peace is a condition to yearn for
To dream for
To vision
Imagine,

If we were sitting on our durable *b's*
We wouldn't have the song with nearly so much
Passion.

So move toward peace
Bless us toward peace
Leave toward peace --
Take the dream of peace with you wherever you go
And ache for it,

Ache for it so much
It will have to happen because it will not let you go.

You angels of mercy
Do not relieve us of the hunger angst yearning desire lust
We protect like a double helix of identity
For peace
Integration;

Come together
Right now
Toward shalom.

Truly by Michael Getty

                    a beacon
               spacious
          mystery
will be the great name

                                        truly

The slow in-breath   will
     enliven
     signs
               for you
          in strangers' eyes
     in the thick of struggle
in white-knuckled promises

                                        truly

hear the blessing   silence
     the bended knee
          between
numbered heartbeats
     eternal
     eternal
     eternal

what we bless   is
praise   beauty
up from the well
crown all   in air
splendor-swollen
still   higher, higher
flashing

                              (What is   in a name?
                                   Blessing.)

Words are small
by comparison
songs
broken
Comforts thin
Will they be enough?

Say, *truly*

SHEMA
AND ITS
BLESSINGS

Dialogue with the Divine

by Jacqueline Jules

When I petition,
I'm on my knees, bruised
by the hardness of the floor.

I'm an Israelite,
obsessed by the squish
of mud under my sandals,
ignoring the Red Sea,
miraculously parted.

When I praise,
I'm on my feet, billowing
like clouds in a sapphire sky.

I'm Miriam
holding a tambourine,
dancing in the desert, grateful
for the smallest excuse
to sing.

Every Creature Prays by Ty Rocker

Do the fullest winds not begin Nature's sermon
by harmonizing with the deepest valleys,
composing an ancient,
whispering cry?
Do you think that the moon doesn't shout
its loudest appreciation
at night in return for the sun's illumination?
Do the trees not worship in the summer,
then precede to roll up their prayer mats in the fall?
Does the ocean not send multitudes of waves
to crash onto Her sands in continuous,
bowing motions?
Do the wild salmon not get so drunk with the Divine
and fling themselves upstream in attempt to become intimate
with Nature's sacred sobriety?
Did you know that once the first snow melts,
Her praised name can be heard from every woodland,
marsh,
peak,
and range?
The rivers chant hymns as they continue to feed on
        newly thawed glacial spirit.
Oh! And the Groundhog!
Once he awakens from his sleepy slumber
His prayers are heard and commended across the Mighty Plains,
        and far into certain forests!
Do sparrows not sing to Her in the early hours of the morning
        before you even awaken?
Of course they do you fool!
You're not the only one that prays!

Evening Call to Prayer

by Stacey Zisook Robinson

I heard the thunder,
Smelled the gathering ozone and wind.
And I heard the crackle of fire that danced,
A flickerflame of heat and light.
And I heard the trembling earth
that rolled, before it settled again,
into its infinite rhythms
of slow and time.
I heard a psalm --
a hymn to God
in the thunder,
in the fire
in the pitch of the earth.
And into the quiet that bordered
the very edges of that psalm,
I heard stillness,
A voice that whispered to me,
that sang a benediction to me,
that called me to pray.

Go the Juggler by Adam D. Fisher

WAY TO GO GOD
Hot stuff!
God, You made all these people,
in different shapes, sizes,
colors, (I especially like
that blonde over there.),
not to mention
all those personalities;
yet, each one in your image.
Quite a trick!
Way to go, God!

The Lord is My Forester by Neal Whitman

not
in
the trees
but between
Beauty is revealed
the Earth spins but is not a blur
Day and Night are continuous
neither one intrudes
each defers
co-joined
in
shade

The Beginning by Rachel Kann

If you can find stillness,
The jasmine will night-bloom in your direction,
And the breeze
Will carry its sacred exhalation of perfume
Toward you.

Breathe,
The moon will cascade waves of radiance
Downward,
Drop her silver robes,
Glow.

You will awaken,
Overtaken by a love
That asks no permission,

Golden particles rising
Beneath your skin.

All of existence
Longs to be an offering.
Eternity is a constant whisper
Wishing to be listened to.

This is the beginning.
This is only the beginning.
Let it in.

Ahavat Olam by Cantor Abbe Lyons

Eternal love
always was
before I came into this world
that love was there
always will be there
no matter what I do, think, experience
that love is available
all I have to do is open my heart for just a fraction of a second
step into the flow
love and beloved
love and be loved

Ahavat Olam – Love of the World

Somewhere on earth, every minute
hundreds of people are opening their hearts
every moment
someone is committing an act of love
every minute I am awake
is a minute when I could be that someone
keeping the continuous love flowing
the living current
the love of the world
Ahavat Olam

Ahavat Olam by John Reinhart

abstract

love
distant

people

how hard
it
is
to love

people
around you

being human

do the goddamn
good

yourself

no
abstract notions

of
what
it means

human
being

Ahavat Olam by Rabbi Andra Greenwald

I know You love me, Lord of Lords,
And that's how it should be.
But, other lovers professed love
Then took their leave of me.
Your steadfastness and constancy
Have taught me how to trust--
Your Torah demonstrating that
You're true and kind and just.
Each day Your gifts enchant me;
I can't count all that you bring.
Your blessings overwhelm me
(I don't even need a ring).
I'm graced by all Your teachings
And repeat throughout the day
Your mitzvot in the morning
And at evening when I pray.
Your words, they bring me comfort
As I go to bed at night.
You bless me as I rise at dawn
And bask in Your sun's light.
Please never take Your love from me
And all those in Your care.
Praised are You, my loving G-d,
Whose love is everywhere.

Snowbush by Rachel Berghash

Saying Sh'ma before sleep,
an unknown, warm and gentle touch
under my left arm, I lifted myself up and clung
to a tender body without form or image,
and something in me acquiesced
and whispered yes, like the seed of a snowbush,
dormant in the soil for centuries, that cracks open
from the heat of a forest fire,
and blooms.

V'ahavta   by Aurora Levins Morales

Say these words when you lie down and when you rise up,
when you go out and when you return. In times of mourning
and in times of joy. Inscribe them on your doorposts,
embroider them on your garments, tattoo them on your shoulders,
teach them to your children, your neighbors, your enemies,
recite them in your sleep, here in the cruel shadow of empire:
Another world is possible.

Thus spoke the prophet Roque Dalton:
All together they have more death than we,
but all together, we have more life than they.
There is more bloody death in their hands
than we could ever wield, unless
we lay down our souls to become them,
and then we will lose everything. So instead,

imagine winning. This is your sacred task.
This is your power. Imagine
every detail of winning, the exact smell of the summer streets
in which no one has been shot, the muscles you have never
unclenched from worry, gone soft as newborn skin,
the sparkling taste of food when we know
that no one on earth is hungry, that the beggars are fed,
that the old man under the bridge and the woman
wrapping herself in thin sheets in the back seat of a car,
and the children who suck on stones,
nest under a flock of roofs that keep multiplying their shelter.
Lean with all your being towards that day
when the poor of the world shake down a rain of good fortune
out of the heavy clouds, and justice rolls down like waters.

Defend the world in which we win as if it were your child.
It is your child.
Defend it as if it were your lover.
It is your lover.

When you inhale and when you exhale
breathe the possibility of another world
into the 37.2 trillion cells of your body
until it shines with hope.
Then imagine more.

Imagine rape is unimaginable. Imagine war is a scarcely credible rumor
That the crimes of our age, the grotesque inhumanities of greed,
the sheer and astounding shamelessness of it, the vast fortunes
made by stealing lives, the horrible normalcy it came to have,
is unimaginable to our heirs, the generations of the free.

Don't waver. Don't let despair sink its sharp teeth
Into the throat with which you sing. Escalate your dreams.
Make them burn so fiercely that you can follow them down
any dark alleyway of history and not lose your way.
Make them burn clear as a starry drinking gourd
Over the grim fog of exhaustion, and keep walking.

Hold hands. Share water. Keep imagining.
So that we, and the children of our children's children
may live

EMET: Truth -- Established and Otherwise by Trisha Arlin

There is truth and there is truth.
Emet v'emet.

The world is dreadful and frightening.
The world is persistently delightful.
God is the true lawgiver.
God is an indifferent metaphor.

Stories and psalms and prophecies,
Learning and ritual and tradition,
We accumulate it all and amidst the contradictions
We try to capture truth
Within the knowing and the not knowing,
For our ancestors, ourselves, and our children.

It is amusing and sad and heroic
That we stubbornly persist
In knowing
That which is inherently and permanently
Impossible to know.

Blessed One-ness
We acknowledge our ridiculous insistence
On ultimate truth.
We give thanks for our small portion of it
As true as the Ain Sof,
As true as what we ate for breakfast.

There is truth and there is truth,
Emet v'emet.

Amen.

Manna in the Morning

by Jacqueline Jules

Cook fires,
clothing scraps,
animal dung
have long disappeared
from the desert.
But the story remains:
how the Israelites
fled Pharaoh
under a spiral
of swirling white clouds
as angels swept
stones and snakes
from their path.
For forty years,
Jews followed Moses
with manna-filled bellies,
thirst quenched by
a wondrous wandering well—
the same fountain I sipped
this candle-lit evening
with honeyed challah
and roasted chicken.
Carrying dishes to the sink,
my sandaled feet skip
on a freshly swept floor,
free of snakes and stones.
Tonight, Pharaoh lies drowned
behind me
and I am traveling to Canaan
under a sheltering white cloud,
certain of manna in the morning.

Mysteries of the Bible by J. H. Johns

Forty years in the desert,
huh?
I guess
that's what you get
when you don't lay out
whatever
 it would have cost-
back then-
 to get a Trip Tik.

Mi Chamocha by Rabbi Andra Greenwald

Who is like You, Lord, our G-d?
No one can compare:
Not Spiderman nor Batgirl
Nor "Clark Kent" up in the air.
No one is as awesome,
Bathed in holiness,
Though many worship others
To escape lives in a mess.
Wonder Woman's powerful;
Spiderman can climb a wall,
But, You, our King and Sovereign,
Are mightier than them all.
Your job is doing wonders,
You laid aside our foes;
Even mighty Pharaoh
Succumbed to Your grand blows.
You redeemed us for all ages
And set Your people free,
Not just for all those years gone by;
Today You redeem me.
When you split apart the waters
And we walked upon dry land,
I felt You, as I do each day,
Holding me in Your hand.
We sang Your praises at the sea;
You'll reign throughout all time.
I sing your praises every day,
Superhero Most Sublime.

Miriam's Circle Dance by Rabbi Diane Elliot

Come, women!
follow the circle of my *tof*
lailailailailailailai !
open wide the circles of your throats
and from the *mitzrayim* of the body,
your narrowest places,
send free the sobs and laughter, sighs, groans, screams
four hundred years of swallowed sounds

lailailailailailailai !
stretch your spirits
like pelvic bones in labor,
widening to birth God's light
lunge! squat! spiral!
trace with stamping feet
the mystic circle of inclusion, acknowledgement
and praise

be the circle
expand your circumference
shrink to a single point
ingest this "different breath,"
this gust,
exhilarating,
searing as hot wind
lailailailailailailai !
unleash at last
the devastating longing
that, for all time,
glues us to the holy
lailailailailailailai
One!

Stopping off at a street vendor on a snowy evening by Raoul Izzard

The chestnuts the girl
plucked from the embers
with sooty fingerless mittens
pocket me in toasty-warmth.
The long walk home
just got shorter.

Nothing Archaic about It by Ben Berman

After Rilke

She wakes and cries out with an onslaught
of needs, beckons us like the torso
of Apollo: *You must change your daughter.*

And to hear her tempestuous throes
as we fumble with the snap of her buttons
is to realize how easily change throws

us all off balance – these tattered patterns
of sleep, our quarters cramped into eighths,
the relentless demand to put down

our work, books, forks – not that it doesn't feel right,
but the *right* in *right now* is intensive.
Our ends have never felt so loose. The tight

fit of our best swaddle is tentative
in the fits of her sleep. Even on weekends
we're up before three. Something has to give.

But we hold on – holding her – tired, weakened.
And something else inside of us awakens.

Watch this Space by D.L. Lang

And you will keep Shabbat,
keep it safe from the weekly toil,
and learn to just be.

And I will protect Shabbat,
protect it from the hurry,
and learn to be slow.

And we will guard Shabbat,
guard it against worldly sorrows,
and know true joy.

And it will keep us,
inching towards holiness,
connected,
closer.

Together
we watch this space,
and marvel.

Together,
we enter this space
to be refreshed.

Half A Kaddish by Danny Maseng

Half a *Kaddish*!?
Half?
That's what I get for always being late.
I could have gotten *Barchu* or even (dare I dream?) *Aleinu* -
but no, all I get to offer you is half a *Kaddish*.
I'd love that you should think of me as far more grateful, but
tradition, form, and sequence permit me only half.
Not that the prayer makes any sense, mind you: late as I am - I'm
singing, blessing, praising, glorifying, exalting, extolling, magnifying,
uplifting, and lauding you -
only to find out that you are completely beyond such silliness.
Your rod and your humor comfort me.
My teacher always told me that pointless effort was the greatest of all.
My teacher is long gone and I am still at it:
Stumbling towards you
Half-witted
Half-crazed
More than half way through my life:
May your name keep growing in my heart
and in the hearts of all the seekers of your name.
May we be increased and blessed
and may our eyes be upraised to really see
the glory of your kingdom
in our half-trashed Eden
swiftly,
Uvizman Kariv,
and even sooner,
and let us say

T'FILAH

In Praise of Doubt   by Stacey Zisook Robinson

I find God in my doubt,
In the struggle to
Be
The absolute best of me,
And in my fear
That I find only my
Worst.
I wrestle,
and am restless
and I wander, rootless,
exiled,
barricaded by my silence.
God of Hosts
and Light
and Mercy--
God of the desert
and unseen edges--
God of my devotion
and my rebellion:
Open my lips
That I may declare your praise.

All of This Outrageous Beauty

by Rachel Kann

Even in the very act of contraction,
You long to be expansive.

It feels like
Life is trying to drown you,
Choke you out,
Like life is a formidable opponent,
Like shaking your foundation,
Like breaking you open,
Like *holy holy holy.*

Step into the meadow.
Listen to the sycamore
Creak in heavy wind,
Breathe.

Think on the bravery of the seed:
It cracks open
Without even knowing
What it will one day be.

You are glorious
Not in spite of exile, rather,
Because of the struggle.

This merciful universe
Keeps delivering opportunities
To dig in the dirt,
To work.

Creation is built of desire.
If you experience longing as discomfort,
Hunger as suffering,
How will you be able to create?
What will you do

With all of this outrageous beauty?

Amidah by Rabbi Andra Greenwald

Here I stand, in front of You,
My lips proclaim Your praise.
I wish I could just sit and pray,
This was one of those days.
My back is sore, I worked all day,
My feet both scream at me.
But if standing's what You truly want,
I'll lift myself for Thee.
You recall the deeds of those gone by:
My Fathers and my Mothers.
You sustain the living, love those who sleep,
And support so many others.
Faithful are You giving life to the dead;
Great is Your saving power.
But the service grows long and it is late,
Can we limit this to an hour?
Please add holiness to our lives,
Let the Torah be our portion,
And might You send it UPS--
My spine's in a contortion.
Accept our prayer as lovingly
As we offer it to You;
Please let us know when it gets there
And if postage is due.
Return to Zion, Lord our G-d,
And take us with You there.

Shield each of us along the trek;
Please keep us in Your care.
May each of us give thanks to You,
Hashem, You help and save.
We hope these words will protect us
In case we misbehave.
Grant peace to all of Israel;
By Your grace we all feel blessed.
I'd like to sit down now, my G-d,
I need my Sabbath rest.

Precarious Grace by Stacey Zisook Robinson

We stand,
with precarious grace,
in a place
crowded with
ghosts and
the twisted fringes
of obligation
and joy.
It is a
tightrope walk
through dusty echoes
that keeps us
on our
toes.
And so we walk,
boundless,
hesitant -
yes, both at once -
through a world
blazing
with the fire of
wonder and a bit
ink on parchment,
carrying our ghosts,
carrying our fringes.
And just so, we
reach a distant
shore
and dance.

Thankfulness Prayer by Don Schaeffer

Thank You God for giving us
a brain with two hearts
and for our bicuspid day:
darkness dimming logic
nourishing mystery
out of which we love You,
and light to nourish vision,
diminish You, making us temporarily
free.

Softer Than Silence by Harris Gardner

Hear my loud silence, oh Lord!
At its center is the small cry.
Beneath its layers, find my prayer.

The chazzan has a voice
That soars to the world's roof.
My rabbi's chants are like paired
Pianos playing Mendelssohn,
Wisdom crowns her knowing air.

An aperture is in my heart.
Part is opaque; the other, clear.
Sometimes, the voice takes refuge there
To impart inscrutable wonders.

Sometimes, it reigns in reticence.
It has that right when one peers in.
Often, the best advice is none.
In mute amazement, the voice sprouts ears
To hear questions in the percussion.

Answers grow wings in stillness.
The window only needs to be slightly ajar,
And the replies fly out
To cohere with unfettered prayer.

Get the Cliff Notes by Sy Roth

Failed to read the signs--
their poetry eluded me
creatures that fell to the wayside,
an incongruous entanglement
became bent and twisted
things arranged senselessly.

Their quatrains, sestets, sesquipedalian silliness,
fell still
into unearthly mutes,
soulless dybbuks wanting reanimation
trapped in their own morass.

Their words skip along the page
an amalgam of nonsense
sustenance sought in interpretation,
but they are elusive.

Give me the Cliff Notes
show me Waze
to navigate through roads lost in a darkened wood
so I know which to follow,
which to ignore.
which to warn others,
which to fling clumps of shit at
and which to bless with the fringes of a tallit.

Elohai N'tzor by John Reinhart

Dawning light of grace
speaking in the stillness
forgotten between bursts
of neon and promise,
grant me strength of patience
for my work yet undone.

ALEINU /
KADDISH

Aleynu by Rabbi Diane Elliot

Aleynu....
It is up to us.
What are we up to,
Here, together?
Shall we rise
to the occasion?
The way we are,
here together,
is the contradiction
to all that is fearful,
constricted,
stuck and stunted,
shunned and shunted.
Can you carry
this way you are,
here, right now,
this aliveness,
this delighted
Presence,
outside these sacred walls,
beyond this blessed day,
to bless each day
with the loving of the One
Who loves
each one
of us
into being?

Writ on: A Kaddish Prayer

by Janet Bowdan

The children at the littoral edge
write their names for the sheer pleasure
of being able to do so
scooping it out in wet sand
patting it into shape
first name the first they learn to write.
Nobody writes "platypus" in the sand
or "strawberry"; nobody writes that
unless it's their name—like "Cookie."
The older ones draw hearts
around the addition: x + y, xx + xy,
xx + xx, all those kisses, I heart U
the big heart in the hot sand.
The proclamation's the important part,
not how long it will last. You
remember Cookie, how she was there
and then not there, like sand drawn
out from under your feet by the waves.
If you write the name and dig a moat
to protect it, if you build a wall with the sand
and then a castle, if the ocean comes in,
you can always write the name again,
engrain it there on the beach
at the edge of the world.

L'Dor Vador by Ben Berman

For my grandmother, who died a few hours
after my daughter was born.

She would have claimed that God was granting
us a deep and spiritual bond, one final
connection between generations.

But for the next few days I'd be folding
monkey blankies and thinking of shrouds;
felt almost giddy at the funeral

when I saw distant cousins and shared
my good news. My heart would suddenly throb
and I couldn't tell if I'd just shuddered

with grief or joy or a tangling of both,
everyone whispering their *congrats*
and *condolences* in the same breath.

Rebecca by Nancy Shiffrin

"Be Somebody!" you demanded opening
the dresser drawer pulling out deep auburn plaits
recalling first haircut first attempt at fashion
you painted my nails bright red
gave me the ruby I dropped down a drain
I still have your pearls your cameo

Zeyde called you "Becky
Becky *shah*! Becky commere!"
Cousin Bonnie called you "Gramma"
you called me "*goyische kopf*" fretted
I might change my name
"*ess mein kind*" you coaxed
though I was carsick from the ride to Brooklyn
"raw carrots are healthier!" I argued
"too smart for a girl!" you grieved
I still call you *Bobbe*
where is the blanket I kept at your house?
I long to hold it under my chin

they say you wanted an abortion
I imagine you shuddering on the table
vulnerable tissue exposed worrying
"If I die will Yetta remember which child
can't drink milk which needs vaccination?"
you rode out to the strange land
glorious tresses shining
veiled for husband's approach
crouched to birth the nations

I consult your spirit as I never could your flesh
about work words what to wear whom to marry
your tears smile back through the mirror
I hear you singing in the Russian town of your nativit
Rebecca! a big jolly girl holding hands
with a lover feet clattering on cobbled streets
something warm caresses you
brushes and braids your luxurious hair

When I visit my mother, we look for things by Ellen Lewis

When I visit my mother, we look for things.
She can't find her purse, a hearing aid, sunglasses, a photo album.
And I wonder, how can she lose so many things
Living in one small room.

Today it was some papers.
They were once in a box under the bed somewhere, she remembers
And on the closet shelf somewhere else
She can picture the box, but she cannot find it in this place.

You girls, when you packed up my house,
There were so many papers,
Maybe you put them somewhere
Maybe you threw them out.

The accusation hangs passively in the air.
I think of my old baseball card collection,
The 1961 Yankees who captured my heart
And her insistence that she did not throw them away.

So much gets lost over the years.
"When my daughter comes to visit," my mother tells her friend,
"She always says, 'What are we looking for today?'"
And we both laugh.

We Want to Know Why by Jacqueline Jules

Like the animals in Noah's ark
Everything walks by its mate.
There is no Light without Dark.
No Large without Small.

A front and a back to everything.
Hard, Soft. Hot, Cold. Healthy, Sick.

Still, we want to know why

Up is defined by Down.

Joy sits on a seesaw with Grief.

We are Moses on the mountain
begging to behold a Presence,
allowed only a glimpse
as we cower in the cleft of a rock.

Humbled, we climb down,
stone tablets clutched to our chest,
lay them tenderly in the tabernacle
to carry on weary shoulders,
through years in the wilderness,
always pining for the Divine Face
we won't be permitted to see.

The Grand Preparation by Ty Rocker

It seems to be mechanic,
Infused within us, our world programmed to prepare:

Summer over months ago, every incessant ray of the Sun knows it,
The winds must chill, becoming harder--
      they aren't winds anymore but rather blocks of frigid and solid cold.
And then nature's classic role: the leaves fall, the apples picked,
      the trees undress themselves,
      arranging for a traumatic sexual endeavor.
But a subjective truth is pollinated among us.
We will grow layers of clothing to protect
from these hurdled blocks of numbness,
And the squirrels will gather nuts and burrow deep within their nests;
      they are joylessly content with the Sun's absence.
The Sun is also mourning, it will kiss this part of the world goodbye,
      to return again in later months. We shall kiss her too,
      we will miss her, and her voluntary protection.
Some toil with thumbs on heavily blanketed
couches in indoor abodes, drinking coffee or tea,
      or whatever beverage the West is now addicted to.
An innate, unexplainable instinct causes us to become more susceptible
      to emotion, or maybe we overanalyze during these longer months,
      to compensate for the lack of fresh memories; We dwell.
It is undeniable that, like molecules, families disperse during the summer,
but this time! oh this time, we recongregate to ensure warmth
      in these times of need. The People, the Sun hears,
      measure their happiness in lesser units than that when she is around.

For in a sunflower field, on the other side of the world,
      Gabriel pleads to Her on his decrepit knees,
      "Come back mother, you are missed."

For the Life of Me by Neal Whitman

I
don't
hear well
in darkness,
nor do I listen
as well as when I am alone.
That is why now we rise and fall
like the ocean swell,
grieve as one –
Kaddish
be
One.

CLOSING

to the poet/paytan*
of Adon Olam by Rabbi James Stone Goodman

Eternal ruler
Master of the universe
Who reigned
Before everything.

Neo platonic shift
Attached above
Your hands lifted
Waiting --

Mystery poet
You were the best
Of the poets alone and
Scorned.

Philosophy and loneliness
Melting
First G*d was
G*d is G*d will be

Then the shift
From philosophy to
Personal
Head and heart:

Into Your hands I entrust my spirit
When I lie when I rise up
With my spirit my body too
G*d is with me I shall not fear.

You led with mind
Followed with heart.

*legend: Adon Olam from Ibn Gabirol, 11th c.

Dear Master of the Universe,

by Seree Cohen Zohar

I try imagining: how does it feel
to be Adon Olam, to 'disappear'
some of your awesomeness,
make space for us?
I should've been singing along
with intent: instead,
distracted by this ponder-worthy thought,
I sought out the wise Ana-
gram-generator:
    "Fiesta thus nevermore!"
I get it: the selfie preparty over,
you got down to tachless.
And once you had us
where you wanted us,
smack in the middle of your olam,
did you not face-palm with a mighty "oy?"
[Yiddish your true mama-loshen]
stunned at your finite creatures
stirring infinite trouble?
"Yes!" wise Ana supplied, "For is 'long-of-nostrils'
not an aptly masterful trait,
as it is said:
    "He: Forte – Tseuris Maven"?
I imagine your concurrent sigh-chuckle:
though we have end
and you do not, don't we give you
a good run for your money!
Yet, at the end of our day,
what mastery, this:
your persistent belief in us,
for into your hand we commit our souls,
fetal in our minuteness,
massive in your trust.

Adon Olam by Rabbi Yael Saidoff

Caretaker of the world,
Before we were here to acknowledge You,
Your presence dwelled in the vastness of time.
Eternity ebbed and flowed,
and formless space stood still.
All of the universe's potential was held in Your hand.
And then you thought, "How precious is existence!
How right it is to be free!"
But how can I bestow the freedom of infinity?
Form is limited by beginning and end."
An aching longing became intent,
And then a plan, and then a blueprint,
A map of existence that led to Creation,
And back to The Source of all Life.
Then you placed in each a spark.
A light just bright enough to illuminate the map.
Lovingly you watch, even to this day,
The beings that You keep in the warmth of Your grace.
And every night when Your creations lay down to rest,
You place them in the palm of Your hand,
And whisper in their ears, "Infinity."

Between the Braids by Bracha Goetz

What's in the spaces between the braids
Of these new challahs I just made?
How much of me is hidden there?
Between the braids my thoughts appear.

"Shabbos Kodesh...Shabbos Kodesh,"
My lips whisper, hands knead the dough.
Let me see my work is holy,
Raising high what seems so low.

I've heard that Sarah, our first mother,
Once had the right recipe.
What happened to it through the years -
Is there a copy left for me?

"Shabbos Kodesh...Shabbos Kodesh,"
My lips whisper, hands knead the dough.
Let me see my work is holy,
Open my eyes, so I can grow.

On Friday night, my husband
Makes a blessing, and I know
Just what's inside those challahs -
Though I wouldn't tell him so.

He cuts them up, we eat them,
And I can't help but smile,
For all that work, I used to think,
They last such a short while.

But this time - I see what's left -
I know what's hidden there.
In the empty spaces between the braids -
That's where my thoughts appear.

When every crumb,
Has vanished from
The challahs that I made,
What will remain?
Just, my secret prayers,
Offered up between the braids.

About the Contributors

Trisha Arlin, writer, performer and student of prayer in Brooklyn, NY, is a part-time rabbinic student at the Academy of Jewish Religion. Trisha was Liturgist-In-Residence during the National Havurah Committee 2014 Summer Institute. *Place Yourself*, a collection of new liturgy and kavannot, will be published by Dimus Parrhesia Press. Trisha's work is published online at triganza.blogspot.com, RitualWell.org and OpenSiddur.org.

Rachel Berghash, CSW, was born in Jerusalem. She has published a memoir, *Half the House, My Life In and Out of Jerusalem,* Sunstone Press. Her poetry and poetry translations have appeared in numerous literary magazines and anthologies, including *Chicago Review, Christianity and Literature, The Comstock Review, Psychoanalytic Perspectives, Colorado Review, Jewish Currents,* and *The Forward Magazine.* In 2009 her poetry was nominated for the Pushcart Prize in poetry by *The Comstock Review.*

Ben Berman's first book, *Strange Borderlands*, won the 2014 Peace Corps Award for Best Book of Poetry and was a finalist for the Massachusetts Book Awards. His second collection, *Figuring in the Figure,* is forthcoming from Able Muse Press. He currently teaches in the Boston area, where he lives with his wife and daughters and attends Temple Reyim where the Rabbi just happens to be his brother.

Janet Bowdan's poems have appeared in journals including *APR, Slope, Crazyhorse, Verse, Free State Review* and *Peacock Journal,* and in *Best American Poetry 2000* and *Poetry Daily.* She edits *Common Ground Review* and teaches at Western New England University. She was raised not exactly orthodox and met her husband because the rebbitzin played violin next to her mother. She lives in Northampton, Massachusetts, with her husband, son, and sometimes a lovely stepdaughter or two.

Leonard Cohen (September 21, 1934 – November 7, 2016) was a Canadian singer, songwriter, musician, poet, novelist, and painter. He was inducted into the Canadian Music Hall of Fame, the Canadian Songwriters Hall of Fame, and the Rock and Roll Hall of Fame. He was a Companion of the Order of Canada, the nation's highest civilian honor. In 2011, Cohen received one of the Prince of Asturias Awards for literature and the ninth Glenn Gould Prize.

Rabbi Diane Elliot inspires her students to develop a nourishing and deeply felt Jewish practice through meditation, movement, and nuanced interpretations of sacred text. A spiritual director in private practice, she teaches and leads retreats nationally through ALEPH Alliance for Jewish Renewal (www.aleph.org) and has recently published *This Is the Day, Ha-Yom Yom, Poems inspired by the practice of counting the Omer* (Hadassa Word Press).

Adam D. Fisher's four books of poems are: *Rooms, Airy Rooms,* (Writers Ink Press and Cross Cultural Communications in cooperation with Behrman House), *Dancing Alone,* (Birnham Wood/Long Island Quarterly), *Enough to Stop the Heart,* (Writers Ink Press) and *Hanging Out With God* (Writers Ink Press). He was the Poetry Editor of the quarterly Journal of the Central Conference of American Rabbis from 2006-14. He is Rabbi Emeritus of Temple Isaiah, Stony Brook, NY.

Harris Gardner's credits include *The Harvard Review; Midstream; Fulcrum; Chest* and over fifty more, in U.S. and international journals. He has three published collections and co-founded Tapestry of Voices with Lainie Senechal (1999-Pres.). He also co-founded, with Lainie Senechal, Boston National Poetry Month Festival in 2001. He received the Ibbetson Street Press Life Time Achievement Award in 2015 as well as a citation from the Massachusetts House of Representatives in 2015.

Michael Getty is a writer who lives with his husband in St. Louis, Missouri. He completed the Davennen Leadership Training Institute (DLTI) in 2016, and his poetry has appeared in publications such as *The Healing Muse, The Road Not Taken,* and *The Aurorean.*

Bracha Goetz is the author of 36 Jewish children's books, including *The Invisible Book, Aliza in MitzvahLand,* and *Let's Appreciate Everyone!* Her new candid memoir is *Searching for God in the Garbage.*

Rabbi James Stone Goodman serves Neve Shalom Congregation and the Central Reform Congregation, in St. Louis, Missouri. He performs with several musical groups, integrating story and music in a performance art form. In addition to rabbinical training, he has an MFA in creative writing from the University of Missouri-St. Louis. Rabbi Goodman's special field of expertise is the Kabbalah, Jewish mysticism, on which he writes and lectures widely.

Andra Greenwald is the mother of three wonderful girls and is married to her best friend. She is a Licensed Clinical Social Worker and an ordained rabbi. Andra won her first poetry contest while at a Jewish day camp in 1959 and has been waiting to add to that list of awards ever since. She loves people, writing and teaching and strives to make the world better one life at a time.

I.B. (Bunny) Iskov is the Founder of The Ontario Poetry Society, www.theontariopoetrysociety.ca. Bunny has won a few contest prizes and she has several poetry collections. Bunny Is the recipient of The 2009 R.A.V.E. Award, as Art Educator / Mentor in the Literary Arts Discipline and most recently, she is the recipient of The Absolutely Fabulous Women Award for Women over 40, 2017 in Arts and Culture.

Raoul Izzard is an English teacher who lives in Barcelona, Spain with his wife and two-year-old son. He loves drinking coffee in the city's numerous bars and cafes when he isn't on daddy duties.

After retiring in 2009, one inspiring writing workshop launched **Joanne Jagoda** of Oakland, California on an unexpected writing trajectory. Her short stories, poetry and nonfiction appear on-line and in print anthologies including *Gemini, Pure Slush, Poetica,* and *Persimmon Tree Magazine.* In 2015, her poem, "Mr. Avocado Man" was nominated for a Pushcart Prize. Joanne continues taking a variety of Bay Area writing classes, enjoys Zumba, traveling and spoiling her seven grandchildren, who call her "Savta."

J. H. Johns "grew up and came of age" while living in East Tennessee and Middle Georgia. Specifically, the two places "responsible" for the writer that he has become are Knoxville, Tennessee and Milledgeville, Georgia.

Jacqueline Jules is the author of three poetry chapbooks, *Field Trip to the Museum, Stronger Than Cleopatra,* and *Itzhak Perlman's Broken String.* Her work has appeared in over 100 publications including *Poetica, Jewish Spectator, Killing the Angel,* and *Imitation Fruit.* She is also the author of 40 books for young readers, including three Sydney Taylor Honor Award winners and two National Jewish Book Award finalists. Visit www.jacquelinejules.com

TEDx Poet **Rachel Kann** has been featured on *Morning Becomes Eclectic* on NPR and as "The Weather" on *Welcome to Night Vale.* She's received accolades including the James Kirkwood Fiction Awards and LA Weekly Awards. She is the winner of Best Overall Production from Rabbit Heart Poetry Film Festival and the 2017 UCLA Extension Writers' Program Instructor of the year. She is currently matriculating toward ordination through Kohenet. Visit her at rachelkann.com

D.L. Lang is the current Poet Laureate of Vallejo, CA. She has authored nine poetry books and one spoken word album. Her poetry has been published in the *Jewish Journal,* and has won awards at various county fairs. Once upon a time she made a film called the *Hebrew Project* and minored in Judaic Studies at the University of Oklahoma. Visit her online at: poetryebook.com

Aurora Levins Morales is an internationally known Puerto Rican Ashkenazi poet, fiction writer and essayist. She's a member of the Jews of Color, Sepharic and Mizrahi Caucus working in partnership with Jewish Voice for Peace, and a regular contributor to its blog, *Unruly.* Her ecojustice podcast *Letters from Earth* airs on Pacifica Radio's *Flashpoints* and her work can be found on Patreon and at www.auroralevinsmorales.com. She lives in a tiny house in Northern California.

Rabbi Ellen Lewis has enjoyed a bi-vocational career as both a rabbi and a psychotherapist. One of the first 20 women ordained a Reform rabbi, she spent 35 years serving synagogues in Dallas, Texas; Summit, NJ (Rabbi Honorata); and Washington, NJ (Rabbi Emerita). Rabbi Lewis is also a certified and licensed modern psychoanalyst. She is in private practice in Bernardsville, NJ, and Manhattan. Rabbi Lewis writes and speaks about the intersection of mind and spirit.

Cantor Abbe Lyons is a Jewish musician and educator. She teaches music theory, Hebrew and nusach in the Aleph Ordination Program and facilitates SpeakChorus Torah with adults and teens. Her cantorate has also included diverse roles on and off the bimah at synagogues, conferences, college campuses, as well as creating innovative music drawing on Jewish sources with her band, RESONATE.

A singer, actor, writer, composer, and playwright, **Danny Maseng** is the spiritual leader of Makom LA in California. Danny's productions, *Wasting Time with Harry Davidowitz*, and *Soul on Fire* have earned him accolades. Danny has just completed *The Passion, the Beauty, and the Heartbreak*, a book about the luminaries of Israeli songwriting. One of the most popular and respected composers of contemporary synagogue music, Danny has performed extensively on stage, television, and film worldwide.

An arsonist by trade, **John Reinhart** lives on a farmlette in Colorado with his wife and children. He is a Frequent Contributor at the Songs of Eretz, member of the Science Fiction Poetry Association, and was awarded the 2016 Horror Writers Association Dark Poetry Scholarship. His chapbook, "encircled," is available from Prolific Press. More of his work is available at www.patreon.com/johnreinhart, and you can connect with him through www.facebook.com/JohnReinhartPoet and twitter.com/JReinhartPoet

Stacey Zisook Robinson is a poet and essayist who lives in Chicago. She works as a Poet/Scholar-in-Residence, creating workshops to explore the connection between poetry, prayer and text. She blogs at staceyzrobinson.blogspot.com, and is a regular contributor to kveller.com, and Reform Judaism blog. Her book, *Dancing in the Palm of God's Hand*, was published in 2015. *Ani T'filla (I am Prayer)* will be published this fall.

Ty Rocker is a 17 year old living in Riverdale, NY, and a junior at SAR High school. He reaches spirituality through nature, self reflection and music. He sings and writes songs on the guitar, has chickens in his backyard, and aspires to be a poetry-writing-organic-famrer when he's older.

Sy Roth is given to simpleminded meanderings that some have deemed noteworthy of publishing in a wide variety of online literary venues. He seeks to find some understanding in the maelstrom of misunderstanding that the world has provided for his ingestion. He spits out lines that he hopes bring clarification to some souls who trip upon them.

Rabbi Yael Saidoff is a spiritual Rabbinic counselor at the American Jewish University (AJU). She has also lectured at AJU on topics including comparative mysticism and character development. Rabbi Saidoff also works as a therapist at Jewish Family Services and has served as Rabbi at Shomrei Torah, Makom Ohr Shalom, and Beit T'shuvah synagogues. She holds degrees in Rabbinics, psychology and neuroscience. She and her partner have two lively kiddos: Maayan and Emet.

Ellen Sander is a poet currently living in Belfast, Maine.

Don Schaeffer has previously published a dozen volumes of poetry, his first in 1996, not counting the experiments with self publishing under the name "Enthalpy Press." He spent a lot of his young adult life hawking books and learning the meaning of vanity. His poetry has appeared in numerous periodicals and has been translated into Chinese for distribution abroad. Don is a habitue of the poetry forum network and has received first prize in the Interboard competition.

Nancy Shiffrin has two collections of poetry available, *The Vast Unknowing* (available at Barnesandnoble.com) and *Game With Variations* (available at unibook.com) Her novel, *Out of the Garden,* is available at Lulu.com accompanied by an essay, *Invoking Anais Nin.* Her play *Allison's War* is also available at Lulu.com.

David Supper trained at Manchester College of Art and Design and has worked in the UK and Israel as a designer. He retrained as an Art Teacher and spent 35 years teaching art in secondary schools ending as Head of a large, thriving art department. Now he writes poetry and paints, his poems have appeared in magazines and anthologies both in the UK and USA. David's paintings have been exhibited in London and the provinces.

Alan Walowitz has been published various places on the web and off. He's a Contributing Editor at *Verse-Virtual, an Online Community Journal of Poetry,* and teaches at Manhattanville College in Purchase, NY and St. John's University in Queens. His chapbook, *Exactly Like Love,* is available from Osedax Press. He can be found on the web at alanwalowitz.com.

Four times nominated for a Pushcart, **Florence Weinberger** has published four books of poetry, a fifth, *Ghost Tattoo,* forthcoming from Tebot Bach. Poems have appeared in *Rattle, River Styx, Miramar, Poet Lore, Comstock Review, Nimrod, Cider Press Review, Poetry East* and numerous anthologies. In 2012, she served as a judge for the PEN Center USA Literary Contest.

Neal Whitman lives in Pacific Grove, California, with his wife Elaine, where his poetry and her photography are inspired by the beauty of the Monterey Peninsula. Neal took up the writing of poetry in transition from a career in medical education where he introduced poetry in the study of medicine. In his so-called "retirement," he is the haiku editor for the weekly online journal, *Pulse: Voices from the Heart of Medicine.*

Seree Cohen Zohar's work is influenced by Australian landscapes and farming in Israel and appears or is forthcoming in print and online venues internationally. She collaborated with Alan Sullivan on a new, accessibly-versified poetic translation of the Psalms of King David.

Acknowledgements

Candle Lighting by I.B. Iskov first appeared in the Passover Literary Supplement of The Canadian Jewish News, 2005 and was also published in Sapphire Seasons, Aeolus House, 2010.

Dolphin Sabbath by Florence Weinberger first appeared in *Deronda Review.*

You'd Sing Too from BOOK OF LONGING by LEONARD COHEN. Copyright © 2006 by Leonard Cohen. Art copyright © 2006 by Leonard Cohen. Reprinted by permission of Harper Collins Publishers.

Aurora Levins Morales, *V'ahavta.* Copyright © 2016 by Aurora Levins Morales. Used with the permission of The Permissions Company, Inc., on behalf of Aurora Levins Morales, www.auroralevinsmorales.com

Manna in the Morning by Jacqueline Jules was previously published online at Scribblers on the Roof, March 2010.

Miriam's Circle Dance by Rabbi Diane Elliot first appeared on www.telshemesh.org

Northing Archaic About it and *L'Dor Vador,* from Ben Berman's book *Figuring in the Figure,* are reprinted here by permission of Able Muse Press.

The Beginning and *All of This Outrageous Beauty* by Rachel Kann first appeared on www.hevria.com

We Want to Know Why first appeared in the chapbook, *Itzhak Perlman's Broken String,* Evening Street Press, 2017 © Jacqueline Jules

Also from Ain't Got No Press

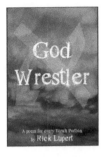 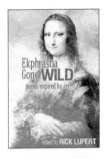 

God Wrestler: A Poem for Every Torah Portion
by Rick Lupert
Ain't Got No Press ~ August, 2017

Ekphrastia Gone Wild: Poems Inspired by Art
edited by Rick Lupert
Ain't Got No Press ~ July, 2013

The Night Goes On All Night: Noir Inspired Poetry
edited by Rick Lupert
Ain't Got No Press ~ November, 2011

A Poet's Haggadah: Passover Through the Eyes of Poets
edited by Rick Lupert
Ain't Got No Press ~ April, 2008

Feeding Holy Cats: The Poet's Experience in Israel
by Rick Lupert
Ain't Got No Press / Cassowary Press ~ May, 2000

I'm a Jew, Are You?: Poems from a Tribal Perspective
by Rick Lupert
Ain't Got No Press / Cassowary Press ~ May, 2000

For more information: www.PoetrySuperHighway.com/agnp

Lightning Source UK Ltd.
Milton Keynes UK
UKHW02f2011040618
323724UK00041B/1833/P